Dinosaur

by Jay Dale

illustrated by Gaston Vanzet

Can you find all the dinosaurs?
I can see 10 dinosaurs. Can you?

This dinosaur is big.

Look at its big *head* and big *teeth*.

This dinosaur is big, too.

It eats *meat*.

Look at its big teeth!

This dinosaur is little.

Look at its little head and little feet.

This dinosaur is little, too.

It eats meat.

Its teeth are very sharp.

Its *claws* are very sharp, too!

This dinosaur is VERY big.
It eats lots and lots of *plants*!
It eats *leaves* from trees, too.
The dinosaur's *neck* is big,
but its head is little.

This dinosaur can run very fast.

Look at it go!

It runs with lots of dinosaurs.

The dinosaurs are all looking for food to eat.

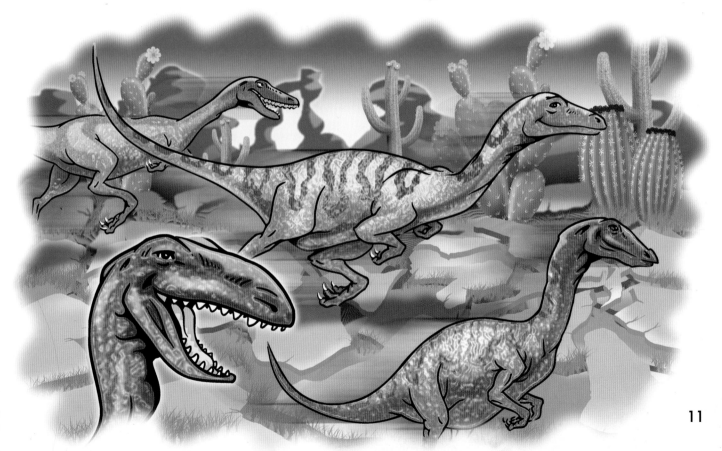

Look at all the *eggs*.
They are in a *nest*.

Look!

A baby dinosaur is coming out.

You can see dinosaur *bones* at a *museum*.

The museum is lots of fun.

You can stay all day.

Come inside and see the dinosaur bones.

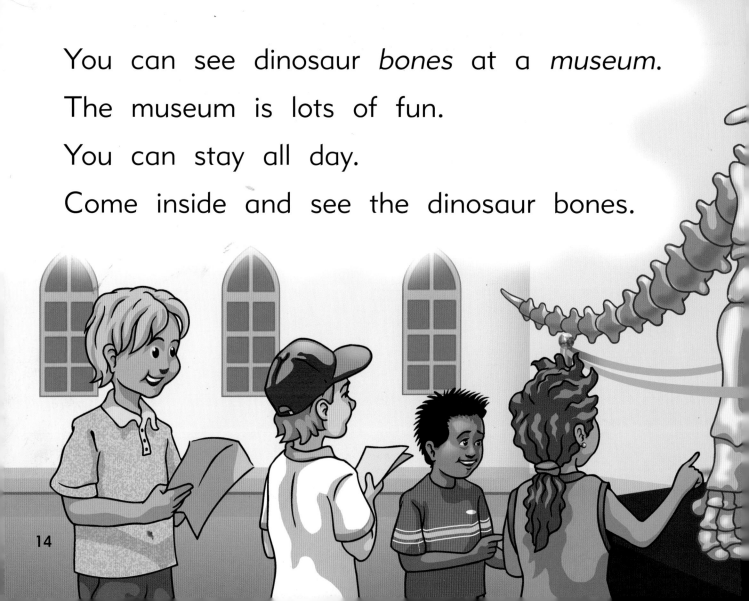

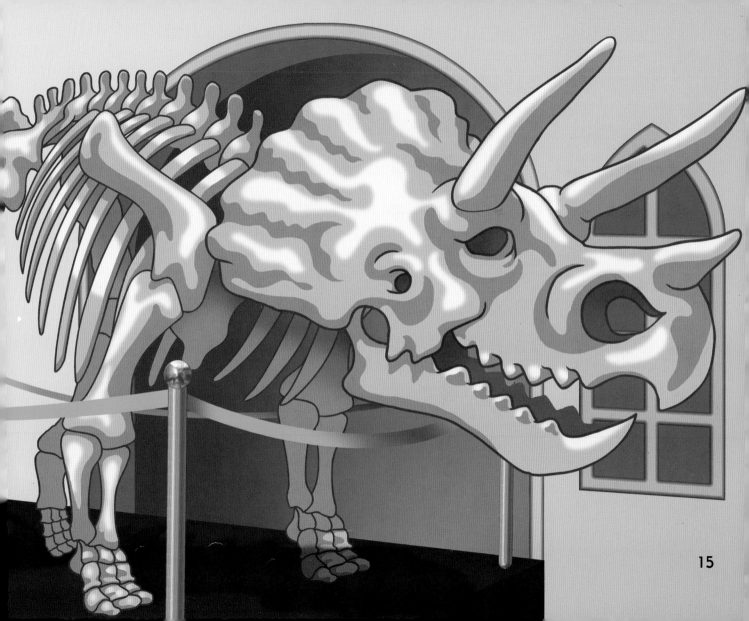

Picture Glossary

bones

head

museum

plants

claws

leaves

neck

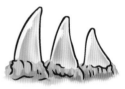
teeth

eggs

meat

nest